Sea Level Rise

by Ashley Kuehl

Consultant: Jordan Stoleru, Science Educator

BEARPORT
PUBLISHING

Minneapolis, Minnesota

Credits
Cover and title page, © Wildcat/Adobe Stock; 4–5 © michelmond/Shutterstock; 7, © MAHATHIR MOHD YASIN/Shutterstock; 9, © Aleksandr Gavrilychev/Shutterstock; 11, © Martin Bergsma/Shutterstock; 13, © Vera NewSib/Shutterstock; 15, © Ion Mes/Shutterstock; 16, © apiguide/Shutterstock; 17, © Harley Kingston/Shutterstock; 18–19, © Harald Lueder/Shutterstock; 21, © WitthayaP/Shutterstock; 23, © Harvepino/Shutterstock; 24–25, © Dima Berlin/iStock; 27, © vgajic/iStock.

Bearport Publishing Company Product Development Team
President: Jen Jenson; Director of Product Development: Spencer Brinker; Managing Editor: Allison Juda; Associate Editor: Naomi Reich; Associate Editor: Tiana Tran; Art Director: Colin O'Dea; Designer: Elena Klinkner; Designer: Kayla Eggert ; Product Development Assistant: Owen Hamlin

STATEMENT ON USAGE OF GENERATIVE ARTIFICIAL INTELLIGENCE
Bearport Publishing remains committed to publishing high-quality nonfiction books. Therefore, we restrict the use of generative AI to ensure accuracy of all text and visual components pertaining to a book's subject. See BearportPublishing.com for details.

Library of Congress Cataloging-in-Publication Data is available at www.loc.gov or upon request from the publisher.

ISBN: 979-8-88916-524-8 (hardcover)
ISBN: 979-8-88916-531-6 (paperback)
ISBN: 979-8-88916-537-8 (ebook)

For more information, write to Bearport Publishing, 5357 Penn Avenue South, Minneapolis, MN 55419.

Contents

Big Storms

Imagine a flood in your neighborhood. Water covers the ground. People have trouble driving through the streets. Water flows into homes.

For many, flooding is a real risk. Earth is seeing more floods than it used to. One reason is because **sea levels** are rising.

Sea level marks the height of the surface of ocean waters. Scientists use it to compare the height of other things. Mountains are measured as a distance above sea level. Valleys can dip lower than this waterline.

Caused by Climate

Sea levels are rising because Earth's **climate** is changing. The patterns of usual weather in places are different than they used to be. Some cities are getting more rain than ever before. Storms are becoming stronger. Many places are heating up.

Weather is what's happening at a certain time. It can be cold or rainy. Climate is the typical weather over years. A place that usually has cool, rainy weather has a cool, rainy climate.

Greenhouse Gases

Why is our climate changing? Human activity is a big reason. People burn **fossil fuels** to make energy. We use them to power our homes and factories. They make most cars and trucks go. But burning fossil fuels lets off **greenhouse gases.**

Carbon dioxide is one greenhouse gas. It comes from burning fossil fuels. **Methane** is another. It is made when waste breaks down. Big farms often let out a lot of methane.

Many factories let out a lot of carbon dioxide.

Greenhouse gases trap heat close to Earth. They act a bit like a blanket keeping warmth around a person. We need some trapped heat around Earth so it is warm enough to live. But more greenhouse gases mean we are trapping more heat. This makes Earth hotter.

A greenhouse is a building used to grow plants. Energy from the sun comes in through its glass walls. Once inside, the light turns to heat and is trapped. Greenhouse gases work to trap heat in a similar way.

Greenhouses can grow plants even during the cold winter.

In Hot Water

A hotter Earth means hotter oceans. About 90 percent of the planet's extra heat is taken in by the oceans. Over time, this makes ocean water heat up. Warmer water takes up more space. All this water has nowhere to go but up. Sea levels rise and push water further onto land.

Earth's oceans are huge. It takes a lot to change their temperature. But from 1901 through 2020, ocean temperatures rose. They got about 1.5 degrees Fahrenheit (0.8 degrees Celsius) hotter.

Melting Ice

A warming climate is also melting Earth's ice. **Glaciers** are huge pieces of ice on land. Some sit on mountaintops. Glaciers cover most of Antarctica and the country Greenland. But glaciers are melting. Melted glacier water flows into the oceans. The added water makes sea levels rise even more.

Light energy from the sun bounces off light-colored objects, such as glaciers. Dark objects, such as ocean water, take sunlight in and make heat. As more glaciers melt, less heat is bounced away from Earth.

The glaciers on Antarctica and Greenland are melting quickly.

Salty Risks

As the sea levels rise, ocean waters flow onto land more often. The salt in this water can cause problems.

Too much salt makes it hard for many plants and animals to live and grow. Ocean water can even make farmland too salty for crops.

Sea turtles make nests on beaches near the oceans. If these beaches flood, sea turtles can't lay eggs. Salty floodwater can also harm any eggs already in nests.

Water on Land

Rising sea levels are also a problem for people. Along the coast, **tides** shift water toward and away from shore every day. When the water is at its furthest inland, it is called high tide. But rising seas are pushing the high tides farther onto land. This causes small floods along the coastline.

Common, minor floods are called nuisance floods. They don't cause much harm. But over time they can damage buildings and streets. Scientists think that the level of these floods will soon become normal sea levels.

In some places, the floodwaters may never roll back into the oceans. Those who live on islands or near the coasts are at risk of seeing their homes go underwater forever.

Some islands are already disappearing under rising waters. People who lived there have been forced to move.

Scientists think some major cities are in danger of permanently flooding soon. Large parts of New Orleans, Miami, and Houston may be underwater by 2100.

Surge!

More heat in the oceans also means more energy for storms. **Hurricanes** start over oceans. They become stronger over warmer waters. So, warmer temperatures from climate change lead to larger and more frequent storms. Along coasts that are already at risk of flooding, that can be a big problem.

Hurricanes start when lots of warm, wet air from the ocean rises up. Cooler air rushes in to replace the rising air. This starts a spinning motion. Eventually, this can become a hurricane.

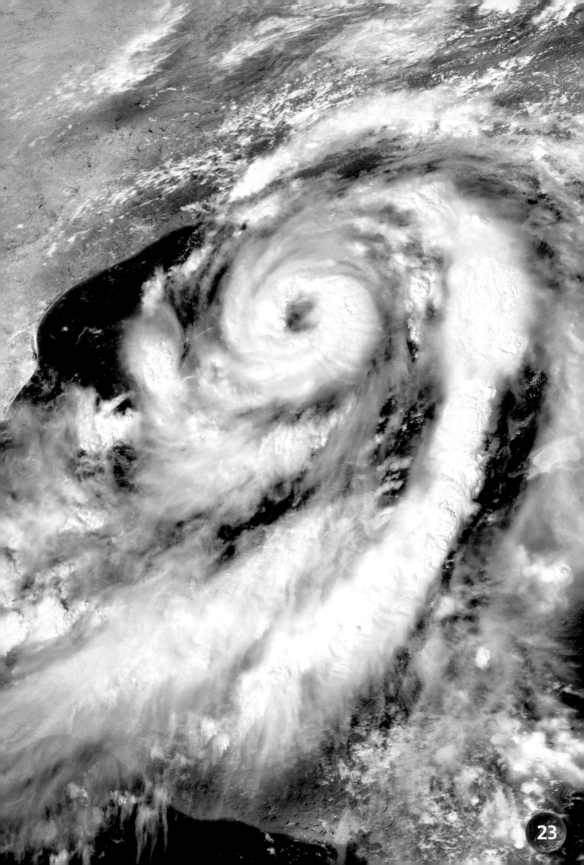

A hurricane's strong winds push water onto land. This is called storm surge. A powerful surge can cause serious flooding. Storm surges can be more dangerous than hurricane winds and rains. They can wash away roads and homes. Some even turn deadly.

Storm surge waters can be more than 30 feet (10 m) high. Surge water often rushes onto land quickly. The fast flooding can kill people who think the danger from a hurricane has passed.

Slowing Climate Change

Humans have caused big changes to Earth's climate. Our actions have raised sea levels. We've sent water rushing inland. But it's not too late to do something. Burning fewer fossil fuels will help slow climate change. Together, we can keep our seas healthier for life in the water and on land.

Scientists are trying to help places hurt by rising sea levels. They help fix broken parts of habitats. They also try to help animals get used to warmer and higher waters.

Bike instead of driving places.

Changing Coastlines

Rising waters will change our coastlines. Major cities may soon be underwater. See where sea levels might be by 2100 in Houston, New Orleans, and Miami.

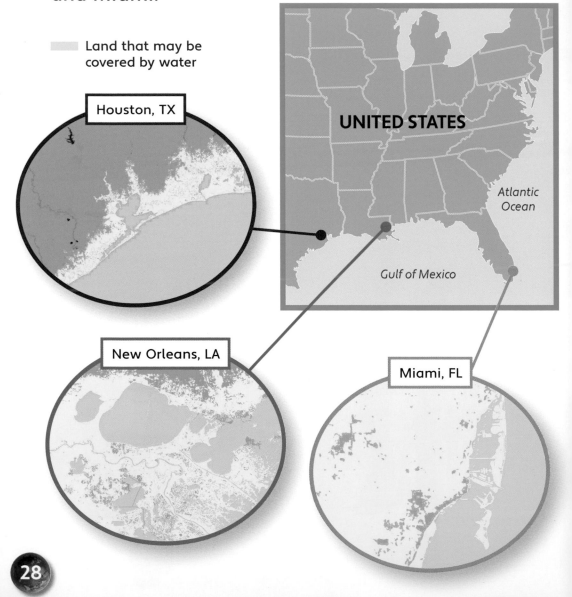

Land that may be covered by water

Houston, TX

UNITED STATES

Atlantic Ocean

Gulf of Mexico

New Orleans, LA

Miami, FL

★ SilverTips for REVIEW

Review what you've learned. Use the text to help you.

Define key terms

climate

greenhouse gases

flood

sea level

fossil fuels

Check for understanding

Why are Earth's oceans getting warmer?

What happens when sea levels rise?

Describe the different reasons waters can flood land and explain the problems of each.

Think deeper

Think about where you live. How might floods affect your neighborhood or town?

★ SilverTips on TEST-TAKING

- **Make a study plan.** Ask your teacher what the test is going to cover. Then, set aside time to study a little bit every day.

- **Read all the questions carefully.** Be sure you know what is being asked.

- **Skip any questions** you don't know how to answer right away. Mark them and come back later if you have time.

Glossary

carbon dioxide a greenhouse gas given off when fossil fuels are burned

climate the typical weather in a place over long periods of time

fossil fuels energy sources, such as coal, oil, and gas, made from the remains of plants and animals that died millions of years ago

glaciers large, slow-moving pieces of ice found on land

greenhouse gases carbon dioxide, methane, and other gases that trap heat around Earth

hurricanes powerful storms with heavy rain and fast winds that form over large bodies of water

methane a greenhouse gas that is made from rotting waste

sea levels the average height of the oceans' surfaces

tides the shift of water on the shore of an ocean or any large body of water

Read More

Bergin, Raymond. *Ocean Life Connections (Life on Earth! Biodiversity Explained).* Minneapolis: Bearport Publishing Company, 2023.

Newman, Patricia. *Planet Ocean: Why We All Need a Healthy Ocean.* Minneapolis: Millbrook Press, 2021.

Owings, Lisa. *Climate Change (It's the End of the World!).* Minneapolis: Bellwether Media, 2020.

Learn More Online

1. Go to **www.factsurfer.com** or scan the QR code below.

2. Enter "**Sea Level Rise**" into the search box.

3. Click on the cover of this book to see a list of websites.

Index

About the Author

Ashley Kuehl is an editor and writer specializing in nonfiction for young people. She lives in Minneapolis, MN.